Transitions
Early Poems: 1979–1989

By Greg Zeck

Dead White Man Press
Fayetteville, Arkansas
2020

Copyright © 2020 by Gregory R. Zeck

All rights reserved.

The following poems in this collection were previously published as indicated:

- "Another Minneapolis Poem," *Moon Magazine,* July 2019, http://moonmagazine.org/greg-zeck-homeless-known-2019-06-29/.
- "Auroral," *Bogg: An Anglo-American Journal,* No. 65 (1987), p. 57.
- "Autumn Colors" and "Two Birds in the News" (latter as "Text & Photo, Page 6B, 17 June 1987"), *Loonfeather: A Magazine of Poetry, Short Prose & Graphics,* Fall/Winter 1990, pp. 33-34.
- "Poem on the Beautiful Hands of Jennifer," *Renegade,* 1989, p. 13.
- "Two Views of Love," *The Spoon River Quarterly,* Fall 1980, p. 64.

ISBN 978-0-578-73319-7

Library of Congress Control Number: 2020915072

Manufactured in the United States of America.

Cover art: Paul Gauguin, French, 1848-1903. *Where Do We Come From? What Are We? Where Are We Going?,* 1897-1898. Oil on canvas: 139.1 x 374.6 cm (54 3/4 x 147 1/2 in). Framed: 171.5 x 406.4 x 8.9 cm (67 1/2 x 160 x 3 1/2 in). Museum of Fine Arts, Boston. Tompkins Collection — Arthur Gordon Tompkins Fund, 36.270. Used with permission.

Typeset in 11 point Sitka Text and other Sitka styles.

For Jennifer, first, last, and always ...
and George T. (Ted) Wright, 1926–2019,
friend and poetic mentor.

A QUICK INTRODUCTION

These 50 poems accumulated through the 1980s. I look back on that decade, when I'd returned to my native Minnesota from college teaching in Michigan, and am both surprised and pleased to see that I had time to write these poems at a time when I was trying to make a living as a freelance business writer. I made a little money, true, but somehow did not lose sight of something more important, the need to express the moment, the place, the touch, the time through which we glide and are elided.

If you don't read much poetry, I hope these poems will be encouragingly accessible to you. I've tried to make them that way, though it's true I have a Ph.D. (University of Texas at Austin, 1974), baggage that might get in your way from time to time (big words, long sentences), as it has got in my way also (the impedimenta of the academic world).

Give it a shot, anyway. See if the poems make sense. See if poetry's not a stretch of the imagination and if stretching isn't fine exercise.

You'll see that the book is divided into three sections, roughly chronological and thematic, and that the names of these sections derive from the famous painting by Paul Gauguin that appears on the cover, "Where Do We Come From? What Are We? Where Are We Going?" With apologies to Mssr. Gauguin, these remain the important questions, don't they? Perhaps poetry can begin to answer them as well as any other art or human effort.

Greg Zeck
Fayetteville, Arkansas
September 2020

CONTENTS

A Quick Introduction iv

I. Where Do We Come From?
Perverse Streak 3
Baby Narcisse 4
Enfants Terribles 6
Formicary 7
Bachelors' Camp 8
Variation on a Theme by Maxim Gorky 10
Dithyramb 11
Twin Views of Tobacco 12
Blood Brothers 13
Eden in Monochrome 15
Physical 17
First Love 18
Dedication 20
Epithalamion 22
Maw Dream 24
Minneapolis Is Empty Now 25
Prayer for a Life without Tools 26
Mote and Beam 28

II. What Are We?
No Muse 33
Auroral 34
Maine Summer 36
Revolutionary 37
In Praise of Privies 38
Another Minneapolis Poem 39
Two Birds in the News 42
Conductor 43
Guinness Book Record Proposed 46
A Birthday Wish for My Father 47
Autumn Colors 49
Something for My Cousin 50

Photos from an Album Never Opened 51
Suburban Sacraments 52

III. Where Are We Going?
Poem in Uncertain Rhythm 57
Meditation for a Chilly February 58
Rx for a Painless Enough Life 60
Ready 61
Navel 62
Night Thoughts 64
Two Views of Love 65
Poem on the Beautiful Hands of Jennifer 66
Walking the Plank 67
Lone Star State 68
Drought and Desire 69
Encounter 70
Szczecin University Choir Storms Holy Cross 71
My Friends the Artists Dream 72
The Lover's First Taste of Extraconnubial Bliss 73
El Rey de Mi Corazon 75
Onan Suite
    1. Seeding the Dark 77
    2. Ecce Homo 79
    3. Look Ma No Hands 81
    4. Transitional 83
    5. Songs My Mother Taught Me 85
    6. Gloria 86
    7. Sweet Solitude 87
Charms of Oblivion 89

Endnotes
Endnotes 90

I. WHERE DO WE COME FROM?

Perverse Streak [Ω]

This perverse streak in me
which only poetry can
exorcise, verse turn aside,
summoning a common bond
or breath, a rhythmic urgency,
a line crossed if not accidentally,
then tripping out of this grim world
eschatalogically: the only way to grace
or immanence being art: the permanence
in change of loving both medium, or word,
and sense, the daily séance in which spirit
is lifted up and audience, faces glowing,
hands trembling, look into the next
world, which is here and now.

[Ω] The Greek omega symbol after a title indicates you will find a note about the poem in the Endnotes, which begin on p. 90.

WHERE DO WE COME FROM?

Baby Narcisse

Looking in the mirror
of ma mère's eyes,
how was I to know
I'd one day be surprised

by what the world would
judge my homeliness?
In the roaring sea
of ma mère's ears,

I was all there was,
all earthly fears
drowned in gurgling
conch music.

In the manufactory
of ma mère's nose,
I came out smelling
like a prima donna rose,

without the worm's curse,
as if on my own.
In the haute cuisine
of ma mère's taste,

I was milkfed lamb
chops and apple,
brazed to a rare
and sweet perfection.

In the catalog of ma
mère's touch, I was
earth and heaven,
mouth and breast —

TRANSITIONS

nothing necessarily
the world's lush
and powerful
would prize.

WHERE DO WE COME FROM?

Enfants Terribles

Five years old, me and Susie McDowell,
my nextdoor neighbor's neighbor,
were sitting down to mock tea.
For this momentous ceremony,
the little card table was set up on the lawn.
The old chipped china was arranged thereupon.
The copper kettle was gleaming on a trivet.

Decked out in white ducks, my hair slicked back,
I poured tap water into her cup, gazed lovestruck
from top to toe at the golden curls, the crinolines,
the patent leather shoes she wore. She smiled,
and I asked if she took sugar. She said she could think
of nothing better. I dropped one lump in Susie's cup,
she asked for two, no, three. In the shade of the Aldrich
Avenue maples, we were enjoying a perfect idyl.

When out the front door like a bat from hell shot
my four-year-old brother Bob, wearing only his BVDs
and a diabolical smile. Susie and I squinted into the sun
and saw Bobby squatting like a dog, dropping his drawers,
and, horror of horrors, before I could jump up and summon
Mom, depositing one lump, no, two, three, four lumps on the
        lawn.

Of course, his hide was tanned for that, and I grit my teeth
and was glad. But, hot tears streaming down my cheeks,
I looked out the window at the empty lawn.
Never never never would she come again.

TRANSITIONS

Formicary

Seven a.m., the first day of creation,
the May sun booming on sidewalk and home,
fires of serenity slash trees and grasses.

Kathleen, my six-year-old sister, stands
on the walk, credulous Kit in white organdy
and veil, holy communion day, first taste
of God on a cracker, black patent pumps,
blonde hair and fair face, wide-eyed
astonishment and open-mouthed wonder.

Ants swarming underfoot, I tell her they're
sacraments, they're snacks. "Amen, amen,
I say unto you," I say, higher than helium,
just ten, crushing ants on my fingertips.
"Take these foodstuffs the Lord has prepared
for you and devoutly wishes you to consume."
Lifting her lips and sticking out her tongue,
Kit squeals, "Praise the Lord, hallelujah!"

Creation chimes like a carillon, cracks
like a clapper mightily swung. "Take ye
and eat ye and remember me, dear sissy!"
Looking her hard in the eye and instructing her
here at our feast of old ants and new innocence.

WHERE DO WE COME FROM?

Bachelors' Camp
For Jennifer

The old Rock River flows like mud.
Grandpa Henry, in hip boots, plaid shirt,
fly in hat band, stands in the current
with his buddy Ford. Their rods
are whipped back over their heads.

Grandma doesn't like it at the bachelors'
fishing camp: the smell of fish guts,
tobacco, whiskey; the whiskery men
swearing fearsomely; Grandpa dragging
Luckys (a two-pack-a-day man here),
gasping emphysemicly for air;
Ford, divorced and guzzling V.O.,
pinching Grandma's bottom.

Like words they can't drag out
in the company of women, hook,
line, and sinker search the river bottom.
Rancid clams, their bait, fish aphrodisiac,
make lines snap, rods stiffen.

Downstream, wading by myself,
I'm thirteen and my breasts ripen.
While Sis, Mom, and Grandma fuss,
preparing supper, I keep my tee-shirt
on, close my eyes, plunge my toes
in the voluptuous slime.

All afternoon, besides catfish
the men catch nothing but hell.
Grandma is yelling she's got
the coals going and wants
the fillets now. In that dumb

TRANSITIONS

communion of fish and man,
wheezing sympathetically,
Grandpa gazes at his simulacrum,
the whiskered mouth, the horny
barbs, and does what needs
to be done: pulls hook
from gullet, cuts off
the head, rips out
the guts and tosses them
into the bush for the crows.

Hands clasped, brow knit,
Grandma spits out grace,
and we eat catfish fillets,
corn on the cob and peas
from the garden. When suddenly,
as the biscuits pass, Grandpa Henry
sputters, fish out of water,
turns blue, chokes on air.
Ford grabs the oxygen, lifts
the cup to his pal's lips, watches
him drink greedily, while I look
off down the river, muddy
and promiscuous as death,
and know I'm a lucky, lucky girl.

WHERE DO WE COME FROM?

Variation on a Theme by Maxim Gorky

All day the boarders go about their business,
soldiers, draymen, servants, and Tartars' wives.
Grandpa and Grandma, too, join in the chorus
cursing and reviling the weird one among us,
the alchemist locked in his dim shuttered room:
the stinks he makes with his acids and bases,
sizzle of lead, demented cackle as he hammers
the base metal of their curses into thin sheets
of beaten gold. Powers of darkness! they chant,
at the keyhole. He must be in league with Satan!

It's only the child among them who goes to the man
in his cluttered room and watches him, untiringly,
at his experiments.

And in the evening, when all else has failed,
sits with him, hour after fading hour, two
bumps on a courtyard log, two brown owls
blending into the late summer sky's strange
transparency, into the earth of burdock,
wormwood, nettle. Sits with him unblinking,
little hand in his great blistered hand, watching
the moon rising above it all, jackdaws cawing
and wheeling, linnets, goldfinches, martins
sweeping into the inhuman night.

Dithyramb Ω

Goddamn, why don't you love
God? little brother Bobby asks.
It's one a.m., he's drunk again,
on the phone. Why don't you love
anybody? Why're you so damn
serious? he says. Why not loosen up?

Remember how we were locked
in the Christmas tree lot box?
I say. I was five, you were four.
You swore we'd never make it out
alive. Some fool had come along
and popped the top on, an old
storage box we were playing in,
a box like mother's womb, you and I.
It was stifling hot, we were hunched
down in a rot of grass and leaves,
there was hardly any air to breathe.
We were down on our knees, I held
your hand, Bobby. I prayed to my
guardian angel to deliver you and me,
and he, an able midwife, all bright
wing and aureole, sped over the box,
flicked off the lid, freed us to live
another day.

Why don't you love Jesus? Bob queries.
Why don't you love me? Who died —
deep in his cups, he hiccups —
on the cross for you and me. I say,
I love the marvels of modern science.
Take vitamin C. I love Sinus Pauling,
Bob says, snorting, and the Pulitzer
Prizes he won.

WHERE DO WE COME FROM?

Twin Views of Tobacco

The last time we saw Remus
he already carried death
within like a baby
in the womb,
like a little skeleton
he was nursing.

Hacking he brought
his hand to mouth,
suckling pig seeking
the tit of the cigarette:

just one more suck
and then one more
and then one more suck,
the whole pack of wolves
at the door at once.

Remus, porcine and all
too human, wanted so
to get back to the sow
that ravens on its children,

gulps them one by one
that they may be reborn,
return to the womb
and nothing.

Sucking on nicotine's
an addiction, Romulus
the surgeon general warns,
and can have adverse
effects like death and
other irreversible events.

Blood Brothers

The gold and ivory
laden heart of Africa
beckons in the blood
of two slashed veins

in the arm — one mine,
one the chieftain's.
When the razor glints,
blood flashes from the vein,

falls drop by drop
into the cup mixed
with tears of pain
and palm wine.

Black man and white man
do not now question
this new complicity,
but rub cuts and drink

up and share trade
secrets; for I will tread
into the beating heart
of my friend's territory,

hunting gold and ivory,
enjoying favor with new
ally, gods' protection
against enemy,

and he will have my
trinkets still (cuckoo
clock lugged from Germany,
shotgun to add to his armory

WHERE DO WE COME FROM?

of spears, a bit of schnapps,
a stethoscope he plays
with now, startled by his
own breathing).

If you betray this
confidence, he says
(as we hang blood
drunk on each other's

neck), may the lion
rend you, the elephant
engulf you, your gun
burst in your

hands and bullets
pierce your brain.
Clasped in his arms
I wish him the same.

TRANSITIONS

Eden in Monochrome ^Ω
In memoriam James Baldwin

Always a stranger in our snowy mist,
black boy, best friend, you passed
through us in high school in a dazzle,
a negative of white on black flesh.

Just two days ago, Cam, you were living,
breathing, your heart beating wildly
as a deer's in a fog of hunters, when
in the fawn skin of your car, bolting
you thought away from us, you spun
on highway ice, leapt the median,
smashed head-on into an oncoming
truck. Cam, my dear, you who
imparted life and motion to me,
your white shadow, your second gear,
you simply ran out of luck. Skull
crushed, brain strewn like seed
on the road, you died, as you lived
among us, unhappily exposed,
hardly knowing what hit you.

All night, last night, not believing
it was real, I cried into my feather
pillow, while today, our principal,
a triple-chinned white man with three
fat white children, maggots of his own,
commanded me to clean your locker.
Ticking off your stuff into a cardboard
box, tick tock, tick tock, I'm ticked
off, as if I'm laying out your body,
readying it to bury, to throw
into a black hole in the stars where
time is not and forgetting forever.

WHERE DO WE COME FROM?

The dead-loss inventory? Your leather
letter jacket hanging, carrier pigeon
pockets crammed with smudged notes
to me; a black-and-white photo gallery
of the fair girls who smiled at you,
sweet as Juicy Fruit, and said no;
our murderously monochrome civics
text that doesn't know this world
is white no longer; your spiral
notebooks wound like nebulae
with tattoos, squiggles; number
two lead pencils chewed nervous
pensively; a pair of once wind
swift running shoes; a slew
of Hershey chocolate wrappers.

All that remains of you, packed
into this box, Cam, black Adam,
phenomenally about to whirl away,
ashes to ashes, dust to dust. Now
that I must, I slip back, on the brink
once more of innocence, into tears,
and on this film, through this grief
wild light, they're buzzing by, black
on white flies, mere negatives, laughing,
touching, about to mate for life:
drosophila about to spew their eggs
into your grave.

Physical

"No signs of impurity,"
the family doctor said,
Doc Leiferman, scribbling
on his chart, when I was just

fourteen. Good God! what
was he looking for? He'd
just shut the door and done
a physical, sampled blood,

urine, and excrement, made
me stoop, then cough,
my balls in his grizzled hand.
"Jesus! Mary! Joseph!"

I ejaculated, in excitement,
a good Catholic lad and glad
to get out of there in one piece.
What if he told the priest?

Had I been suspect? How could
he know? Would it show?
Crossing myself, I crossed
the good physician's threshold,

sped out into the suburban dusk,
and made bold to think several
impure thoughts about his twin
blonde pubescent daughters.

WHERE DO WE COME FROM?

First Love

How was I to know Felicity
had such a crush on me?
We had played together
in the annual musical

at the Holy Angels
Academy, and while I
skipped the boards
a sailor chanting yoho!

yoho! she pounded out
the tunes on her Wurlitzer.
A sweet stack of cupcakes,
she was plain as a pound cake,

freckled, bespectacled, and
knew just what she wanted.
When Felicity asked me
to her senior prom, I swung

for days, pure baffled motion,
in the noose of her question
before I stopped and sipped
punchless punch with her,

schlepped through the pony
and the twist and, treading
her toes, the Tussy two-step.
Under the starlight in her daddy's

drive in my daddy's Olds,
then, we sat talking
of this, that, and the other
nothing, of the vastness

TRANSITIONS

of space, of what filled
the soul, of the angels'
waltzing, till blue
in the freckled face

she took my face
in her practiced hands
and without so much
as a warmup chord,

a peal of laughter
in the ear, a lick
or a nibble, mashed
my mouth with kisses,

mushed my soul
to little pieces, jack
hammered my skull
with all she had,

first love's full volley,
and, after the way in which
I'd been treated, fell back
glassy eyed and sated.

WHERE DO WE COME FROM?

Dedication
For Robert Creeley & Robert Black

Lurching over the lectern,
squinting at the seven
nuns in the first row
through his good eye,

the poet discoursed
on the pleasures
of fucking. Blitzed, goatee
twitching, sat on the stage,

legs dangling over the edge,
lips sucking a butt,
talking in that disjointed
way of his, that jittery

clipped monotone, on
the terrors of writing.
And when he was done
with the reading,

I approached the man,
a book of his words
in hand given by a fellow
sophomore (who'd scribbled

there, "Ah, fond friend, may
poetry remain our citadel"),
and looking direct at the pirate's
patch asked him if he wouldn't

be so good as to bestow
a small favor. Chuckling,
he said yes, why not, of
course, and before he

inscribed his dedication
("For the only
friend this is — with
pleasure Robert

Creeley") bent
down and kissed
the naked nape
of my neck.

WHERE DO WE COME FROM?

Epithalamion

My little brother Bob
loves Liz Taylor, wants
to propose but is too shy,
a guy like him that's been

married three times.
Broker, brother, tinkerer,
spy, may I offer my services
and say, "Oh my, Ms. Taylor

(may I call you Liz?),
you who know a thing
or two about who is
and who's not eligible:

whether or not you're
married today (can we
keep up with you, can
we be sure?), my little

brother, Billy Bob
McGruder, would
very much like, if it
wouldn't be rude or

presumptuous, to take
your paw in holy
matrimony. S'il vous plaît:
no acrimony!"

Imagine the headlines,
the photos too: "Liz to
Marry Umpteenth Time:
Bridegroom a Recluse

TRANSITIONS

Nurse and Satyr." In Reno,
January 22nd, kissing,
faces glowing
like the wedding cake.

WHERE DO WE COME FROM?

Maw Dream

Sentenced to death, by a grisly tribunal,
three black hooded monks with (live) boas
about their necks, I'm told the punishment
fits the crime, which is horribly unimaginable.
I hear the disposal start up, the whir of stainless
titanium alloy blades, the high pitched inescapable
song of my end. When they remove the blindfold,
I blink under the brightest klieg lights imaginable.
The peanut gallery are all in place, munching,
hooting, tootling their kazoos, urging a gradual
slow plunging, inch by inch, into the stench
of the churning sewer. When my eyes only
are left, on top, waggling unrepentantly
like lobster stalks, I beat my breast
with remembered nerve endings
and cry out, "Look, Ma, no hands."

TRANSITIONS

Minneapolis Is Empty Now
For Gerry

Every time I drive by your house, the hulking
green clapboard Loch Ness monster emerges
from the morning mists, brother. How many
times would I stop by, unannounced, dear
alchemist, to find the coffee pot on, you far
gone in the basement, sweating copper
to carry water or developing out of pitch
dark and a pinch of silver photos of naked
women, poring over each line, each curve
of flesh, the grain of light and dark that fed you.

You spoke of the magic of water blessed
by Father Hennepin, the Mississippi, Father
of Waters, and its transformation from gold
to grime along its sprawling course. You marveled
how for a time it had rushed under the Mill City's
mill wheels, crushed the Great Plains grain
and then, polluted, evaporated in the mind
of the nineteen seventies.

Even as we talked and talked, Itasca basked in ice.
The skyscraper lights downtown winked out
one by one, the briefcases walked home.
The Gulf loomed open-mouthed.

Listening still, liking what I hear, brother, I liken
your words to the sweet flow of water over rock
and miss you, brother, in that wooden house,
more than I can say.

WHERE DO WE COME FROM?

Prayer for a Life without Tools

It's the entropy that gets me, Lord,
the irreparable wear of year after year
against the wood skin of this old house.
It's a three-story four-square built in 1913,
and nothing is plumb, level, square anymore.
The proud fifth owner, neglect's blithe inheritor,
I can hear its malevolent breathing, its implacable
roar for more work: more! more! more!

Wherever I walk, the concrete sidewalks spall,
the crabgrass sprawls, the creeping Charlie charges.
Wherever I look, the clapboards scale, eavestroughs
clog, the red roof rots, the chimney sways and totters.
When I listen, the loose stairs squeak, the toilet
seeps, the boiler in the basement bowels cries
for tuning, the radiators hiss, needing bleeding.
Good Christ Jesus who died for us, you name it!

Take this circular saw from my hand, Lord.
Take the paintbrush and pry bar, the hammer
and nails, the scraper and sandpaper, the plane
and chisel and drill. Take away these instruments
of home improvement. Let them pass. Wrest
these tools from me, Lord, let me be. Lop
my hands off, let these powers atrophy. Rend
me limb from limb. Render the fat of my pride
from the meat of my spirit. Let the hammers fly.
Vaporize the planes. Explode the saws
in a hideous combustion.

TRANSITIONS

And when thou hast had thy fill of me,
dear Lord, and my godawful whimpering,
install me in paradise, in mindless ecstasy,
in a condo in the suburbs.

WHERE DO WE COME FROM?

Mote and Beam [n]
"And why beholdest thou the mote that is in thy brother's eye, but perceivest not the beam that is in thine own eye?" — Luke 6:41

Brother, the beam in my muddy eye is as wide as the Missouri. Across it I drive in a rage and a flash the teams of my hypocrisies: insolence, indolence, monstrous pride, petty jealousy, backbiting, dishonesty, intemperance, licentiousness, covetous desire, despairing death in life.

Councilor, the mote of your benevolent blue eye's the spring that feeds my malice, that trickles through my dry mind, quickens my dark rages. This rivulet that now roars in my ears, brother, is the source of my malaise, is the delta to which my ire returns. Know, brother, you lie through your pearl-perfect teeth if you say you're other than virtuous.

So I proclaim from the rooftops the kingdom of your ten-toed sloth, ten-fingered thievishness, tight-bummed priggishness. You, I crow, from my wobbly stand, from the bandbox of my good opinion of myself, you with your soaring drunkenness, intemperance, vanity. You with the sour breath of your jealousy that wavers about my accomplishments, with your impudent appetite for my daughters and my wives. Councilor, the still water of your gonorrheal soul runs deep beneath the kingdom.

This linen of lies I air in public, brother. I soil your name. Whore of Babylon! I cry, pounding the lectern. Gleefully I cry: I err, yea in body and in soul, if I call you, mite, worm, boar, brother, the apple of my eye! The blue mote of your eye is the bull's-eye toward which I blaze the arrow of my invective, toward which my rattlers' venoms fly. Come out of your hiding, Pigshank, Hogsnout; reveal the breath, the true breadth, of your iniquity.

TRANSITIONS

Oh brother, I roar, you take the cake! You take the ape's part in the dance of indelicacies. In the rearview mirror of my laughter, in full public view, you scratch the rear end of your sanctity, anything to get a rise or two, a piece or two of the moral pie of the polity in which you've already stuck your finger.

Wise beyond all others is your name, Councilor! When I say your avarice knows no boundaries, your looting is no less than spectacular, your lewdness known far and wide, your appetites as undiscerning as they are deep, I lie through my broken teeth. I breathe your demise. I shake snake-eyes. In the theater of your ruin I slither off.

II. WHAT ARE WE?

No Muse

No muse is good muse,
says my son, wise guy checking
in on his old man staring at the screen.
Today, long after I've abandoned poetry
(everything I've written frustrating
head ramming, vain gate storming),
after several hours of mortaring
and patching spalled sidewalk,
mowing lawn and raking
and weeding, of seeing there —
in the repair of everyday decay,
the taming of natural impulse —
signs of measurable progress,
I'll return to the screen tired
and refreshed and see here
sprouting suddenly in vivid
green against a black background
the seeds of words that somehow
have slipped through the cracks
and are making a poem.

WHAT ARE WE?

Auroral

Humping the horizon
here he comes
Don Juan
old inamorato
of the dawn.

Crowding bloody
murder
Chanticleer
cock of the
azure walks
in red
blazer.

Fingertips
of blind
rose mauve
lavender
lascivious
Homer fumbles
for her but
she's not there.

Luna
ticks and
twitches in
the south
west sky the
cracked clock's
last shut
eye.

TRANSITIONS

The best
part of waking
up? The sun
of bourbon
in your
cup.

WHAT ARE WE?

Maine Summer
After Ellen Goodman

Labor Day has closed the cottage of the season.
The caffeine of the news now rouses us from sleep.
But what have we to do with floods in Bangladesh
who late were waked by seagulls on the roof, the sun's
slant through the cracked pane of the cottage, or lulled
by waves drumming the island, the languor of Maine
summer? Dawdling forbidden, summering nixed,
we're jump-started to duty, Tom and I and the kids,
and driven out the door, still simmering with dream,
to work and school. Tom kissed, Jo and Teddy stuffed
in the wagon, I sail off into streams of sulky children,
cursing stockbrokers, profane technicians, and remember
sadly what we brought back from Maine — a gull's feather,
a bag of yellow periwinkles, a bottled sandcastle. Nothing
is fair or good alone. I'd like to imagine a connection.
I'd love something of the summer to last longer
than my tan; to grant heart's ease, an even keel;
to buoy the entire city. Shoulder to the wheel,
I drop the kids at school and, hull slicing the drift,
press hard left up the unending canyoned avenue.

Revolutionary

Pieter van Dijk! Even the name is an archetype,
the perfect name for a blushing apple-cheeked
goateed Dutchman, a Rembrandt van Rijn,
six-feet-three of justice-for-all ideology
and chewed string. Pieter, law professor,
ex-seminarian, globetrotter, lecturer: are
you still turning the world upside down?

The last time you wrote it was from the Temple
of Heaven Hotel in Beijing ("Hot spring
in the garden, peaceful and elegant," chimed
the stationery. "You can reserve a room easily
fastly and surly.") Unfortunately, you wrote,
in your tiny, almost Benedictine script,
the Chinese comprehension of both English
and law leaves something to be desired.

Professor van Dijk, Dutch boy, citizen of the world,
you take the high ground in these low times
when the love of money makes the world spin
and wobble toward cultural revolution. Would
you shore us up against our ruin? Then rush
down and stick your finger in the dike.
The flood tides of capital surge, they roar
against our encumbered wills.

WHAT ARE WE?

In Praise of Privies [n]

In the Netherlands, in the mercantile seventeenth century,
privies were rare, for in that low alluvial soil battered
by the North Sea's ocean's fury they soon filled
with water and stopped. Therefore, the chamber
pot was enlisted and what plopped down was
emptied into the canal. The foul odor emitted
from these picturebook-pretty towns
was in some measure alleviated
by the collection in wooden
vessels of the night soil
and barging thereof out
to the countryside for
the benefit of farm and
field. And so, eventually,
as gold and green vegetables,
cabbages, peppers, corn, melons,
the leavings returned to the tables
of the stout burghers as blessings.

Another Minneapolis Poem
After James Wright

1.
January twenty-second, twenty-two below.
Under the Hennepin Avenue bridge, the nameless
and faceless men from God knows where huddle
in their sleeping bags, delirious as winter stars
and brandy. Mummies transported from ancient
dynasties. Monarchs in the teeth of the next north
wind. In the next slipstream of dream, imagine
them breaking from cocoons, fluttering to Mexico.

2.
In the lobby of the city library, across the river,
built bald and anonymous as Ike's dome
in 1959, the bench-warming boozers gather,
black and white and Indian alike. Gray-flannel
brokers come to see about mutual funds;
high school honeys, with blonde hair and mint
fresh breath, research the plight of the urban poor,
hurrying past the men who sit in the sour pit
of their dead men's breath and pan the room
with dead men's eyes.

3.
Lake Street, broad noon. None too soon
the plainclothesmen arrive, in their full-size
late-model Chevies. Looking for action,
the girls have been on the street since dawn.
Soliciting a cop, they'll spend a few days again
in the can. On the cold metal cots, behind steel bars,
they'll close their eyes and see themselves, long-
maned fillies rolling in impossible clover,
whinnying the praises of alfalfa.

WHAT ARE WE?

4.
In lieu of the bottle they give them the crutch.
At dawn, the sun trembling on the horizon,
they stand in line at the mission, leaning on
each other, jerking with the DTs and the cold.
Below zero, when even snake blood freezes,
they stagger up from the river bottoms,
the railroad yards, the trashed buildings;
end up contrite, not quite right in the head,
ready to trade in their arctic heart
for one more stab at Jesus in the dark.

5.
The old Milwaukee Road train depot, from which
I departed as a child, amid hiss of steam and black
porters' raucous cries, shivers in the cold.
In the shadows of the abandoned shed, the finest
pigeon roost in the city, the men and women I pass
in the morning now in the twilight lay out their dirty
bedrolls. The dignity of their suffering makes me look,
in my business suit, in my starched and laundered
universe, superfluous. Without payroll or prospects,
they bring down to the bottom line the plumed human
breath that whitens this soiled world like pigeon droppings.

6.
Some bum, they think, Indian or white,
has murdered the three Indian women,
slit their throats and left them sitting
by the railroad tracks, off the Hiawatha viaduct,
legs spread wide apart. It's a jungle down there,
ever since Father Hennepin, Belgian Franciscan,
floated down the river to civilize the brutes.
Firewater and firearms conspire to tamp them
down. An out-in-the-cold mentality, an on-the-outside-
looking-in fury puts these women on exhibition.

Brothers and sisters, let us pray
we remember our common clay.

7.
Someday, it may not be soon, the great plume
of our human breath will lift us above this
manmade mess, above the money heaps,
the killing towers. Loosed from the mud
of ownership, our bird heart trilling
through our fluted bones, the cold sky
opening to infinity, we'll take possession
of ourselves in flight.

WHAT ARE WE?

Two Birds in the News

The last pure dusky seaside sparrow
died yesterday in captivity in Florida.
These six-inch brown birds once flitted
the east coast marshes near Titusville,
but after the U.S. space program was
launched, at nearby Cape Canaveral,
their habitat was destroyed. "It's
a very, very sad thing to think about,"
said a conservation spokesman
about Orange Band's demise.

In Paris for an air show, our billion
dollar bomber the Blackbird was seen
and admired by huge crowds of Gauls.
Although the display is over, a small
technical problem is delaying its return
to the U.S.A. The hatch is open, see:
the pilot leaning over the nest, eager
to fly, while below in the bomb bay
the technicians have a wrench
in the machinery.

Conductor

1.
In the publican back pew at Holy Cross,
in Minneapolis' Nordeast Polack ghetto,
Grandpa Tony kneels, after confession,
his rope-veined hands worrying the bone
of the rosary. "Son of a bitch!" he mutters,
between Hail Marys. "Life is suffering!"
Bobby and I, his oldest boy's two boys,
dip in and out among the holy water fonts,
swerving like two swallows, spritzing each
other with the sacred ichor, adding,
"And then, Grandpa, you die."

2.
Propped in an oak box, rouged like a whore,
stuffed in his streetcar conductor's uniform,
Grandpa clutches a plastic rosary.
In Polish, the pastor, a crewcut celibate,
intones the litany of the poor man's troubles,
our common obstacles on the way to Golgotha.

3.
Grandpa, since you died on us, some twenty
years ago, what do we know about the conduct
of life, about the proper way to go? "Educated
fools!" you cry at us from the void, arms churning
like a Mill City flour mill, your supersophisticated
fast-track heirs who've been to school and know,
and believe, nothing.

3.
Illegitimate issue of a St. Cloud farmer
and his creamy dairy maid, you were an ornery
bastard all your life and suffered from the sense

WHAT ARE WE?

it was your sin being born that way. Grandma Gertie
would rock you in her arms, her septuagenarian
baby, bland as a potato, telling you, "There,
there, Pop, it's all right, there, there."

4.
Trolling the streets in your black Depression Chevy,
peeling a Polish eagle's eye, you fished each stray
nut and bolt from the gutter. "Shit or get off the pot!"
you'd shout, putting your boys, Dad and Dan and Will,
to work in your backyard junkyard pulling and straightening
rusty nails from your treasures of warped lumber.
Mountains of two-by-fours and rubber tires,
cratefuls of brass fittings, lead and copper pipe
dwarf the boys as you puff off to work on the Central
Avenue line. If by the time you return, on the stroke
of four, they haven't pulled their weight pulling nails,
you'll give them something to remember you by
with stroke after stroke of your leather belt. "Nothing
goes to waste around here!" you crow, at the top
of your lungs at the top of your dungheap.

5.
What kind of thing was that for Dad to do:
flee the ghetto, take a law degree, change his name
from Szczech to Zeck? Yet what legitimate American
could blame him, say he was wrong in this enterprise?
Even you, Grandpa, visiting the suburbs, had to admit
your son was doing fine: a clapboard colonial on a hill,
a swimming pool, a lively if not Polish wife, and four
model Procter & Gamble kids — me and Bobby,
Kit and Jeanne Marie — whose toothpaste
was Crest and whose mouths were washed
with Ivory soap if ever they forgot their station
in this brave new world of the nineteen fifties
and let fly a filthy word.

6.
Oh Grandpa, I stand on the north
bank, your bank, of the river, just
up from where Father Hennepin blessed
the falls and savages, and watch the towers
downtown glitter across the fouled waters.
Behind my back, gay yuppies flit through rehabbed
flour mills' upscale shops. What is your world coming
to, that sober, saving, tight-assed working world
that only Saturday nights at the Polish club Nordeast
or those summer evenings after Kit and J.M. were
married off erupted into whiskey and polkas?
I can see you still, in your gray and red conductor's
uniform, felt hat and striped woolens, making
change as others make love, redeeming your
passengers' filthy quarters, nickels, dimes.

7.
What is the sense of all this *gówno?* Here,
at St. Mary's Cemetery, standing at your snow-
covered grave, I look to you and Grandma Gertie,
lying low, all bone and dirt and worms. Chickadees
burst through the frigid air, a mirror so brittle it might
crack with my breath. Dumb pilgrim, I scatter breadcrumbs
on the snow and, in my own way, pray: Grandpa, bastard
like the rest of us, bit player in the drama of redemption,
you had hell itself to pay for your illegitimacy yet managed
to enjoy yourself occasionally. Now, in the middle of life's
journey, I believe if anything, whatever the end, that life
is suffering and, looking round this cold waste scene,
find you sadly wanting.

WHAT ARE WE?

Guinness Book Record Proposed [12]

Surrounded by five generations of family,
twenty-two children and their infinite spawn,
an illiterate farmer, Kellabhai Navrabhai Rathwa,
proclaims his belief he's lived on this earth
one hundred forty-nine years.

The old man's memory is sharp.
He recalls with an almost crystalline clarity
his boyhood in the remote village where he was born:
how he hustled the buffalo each morning into the village
    commons;
how he harvested rice under the new moons of his youth;
how, crying, wringing her hands, his mother told him
he would have to leave home in the year of the great famine,
eighteen hundred fifty-six.

The patriarch of Borkhad, five hundred miles
southwest of New Delhi, the ancient white-haired Indian
has no recollection of the century's great events:
neither World War One nor World War Two
nor the coming of the Bomb.

A Birthday Wish for My Father

Three quarters of a century
and far away, Father
is seventy-five today.
At home in Minnesota,
I rise up this summer
morning, tea cup in hand,
hot and inscrutable,
and bow to the graven
images of my ancestors
arrayed on the piano.

Like a quick arpeggio,
the photos still surprise:
Father, seventeen,
quiet and confident
in high white collar,
a butterfly, a sixty-fourth
note, about to graduate
from high school
into the higher life,
the stuff and study
of transcendence
in a career as lawyer.
Grandfather, twenty-two
and smiling crookedly
in blue serge and coin
changer, fresh off
the farm, beginning
work as streetcar
conductor. His father
before him in bib
overalls, unabashedly
in harness, behind

WHAT ARE WE?

the plow, scowling
in the furrows.

Seventy-five, seventy-
five! I rise up this
morning angelic, alive,
transparent as air,
without work or worries,
a muted trumpet,
and call my old man
in the outback,
in retirement,
call him Robert,
his earthly name,
and wish him
a luminous wing
and a prayer.

May you enjoy many
happy returns, I say,
Father, till you too fade
and are graven, like
your father and grandfather
before you, part of the ever
rising arpeggio, the unearthly
succession, pianissimo
and purely in our minds.

Autumn Colors

Sweeping through the sumac by the river,
flaming maple, oak, ash, alder, yellow,
scarlet, bronze, hell, night, roller coasting
through the autumn woods, on U.S. 61,
me and my wife singing a medley of idiot
songs: Hi-ho, hi-ho, it's off to work we go
some enchanted evening when the moon
comes over the mountain, when we pause
to catch our breath, stare straight ahead,
bedazzled, at the ruby of the setting sun.

When over the rise from the other side
some suicidal fool in a blue Malibu, passing
on the hill, comes straight at us at 70 mph,
hell bent on metal. Christ God! we scream,
in chorus, we're going to die! And just as I'm
about to turn the wheel, sharply, to the shoulder,
he takes the gravel and we're flying by each other,
a chrome strip away from death.

Pulling over, I allow my wife the luxury of tears
(thirty seconds' worth), the diamond on her finger,
which is forever, glinting. In the rearview mirror
I see our antagonist approaching, and I step out,
boots crunching the dead leaves, and stride
toward him like a tinhorn sheriff, the furious
law in my own two hands, swearing I'll strangle
the idiot. Crabwise, he comes sidling toward
me, a little guy, red-faced and so embarrassed
he could die, in blue jeans and white shirt,
a truce flag, his hands spread out apologetically.

WHAT ARE WE?

Something for My Cousin ♑
Who took her own life

The numbing mumbo-jumbo of the rosary,
led by an old woman remotely family,
batted off St. Bridget's brick and the coffin.
I snoozed but picked up my ears, somehow hoping,
when the goateed priest, half through the mass,
capered to the lectern. Ours, he said, comfortably,
not to question why this dread thing happened
but to know the Lord works in mysterious ways.
Capon! Mumbling of resurrection and eternal life,
he got on with the job, hoisted the chalice, wiped
his dribbling chops, handed out communion, leading
the faithful up faith's candy-coated mountain.

She's nothing to me, either, Father, this dead
woman, my first cousin, ungermane. Am I my
cousin's keeper? She took her own life and she
took her time, ODd on rage when the techno-
philiac quack MDs hooked her at the sanitarium
on a quick and easy answer to her lifelong pains.
Pop one of these sugar-coated miracles three
times a day, between meals, they counseled.
Avoid milk. Avoid confrontations with your mother.

At the ceremony, her mom, grief- or dumbstruck,
choked up, didn't argue with her daughter anymore
but sang, with the crowd, the pop psalm "On Eagle's
Wings," a modern liturgical manifestation of the need
to believe there's something out there waiting for us,
after all. In my cousin's case, it was to be cremation.

Photos from an Album Never Opened

1.
In this album never opened, this haunted
light of childhood broken, I do not see
but with my mind's eye your brown hair
and brown eyes broken against futurity.

2.
Someone's driveway. A flat gray sky.
Our two shadows flattened on asphalt.
What was it I said, or you said, that day,
to cause us to laugh uproariously?

3.
A few dead soldiers on the grass. Potato
chips littering a checked tablecloth. All
afternoon you lolled and tanned, your
body curved like a beachball in the sun.
All afternoon you lay as if on sand,
the blue lake of your future spanking
wave after wave after wave.

4.
Sockets of black shadow under your eyes.
I took this one of you the night before you died.
You peer out grave, drawn, as if already your fate
were known, the dawn hurl you
into flaming noon, vehicle overturn,
body burn. Over and over again
I review the nonexistent film.

WHAT ARE WE?

Suburban Sacraments

Thirty-four years ago today, Della,
you and Harry moved to Richfield.
Mark, your oldest, was a kindergartner,
the others a gleam in your Catholic eyes.

In 1953 the trees were dwarfs. There was
no shade anywhere in that broiling suburb,
no relief from the sun of post-war ambitions.

Richfield, once farmland, was a sea of GI housing,
bounty for mowing down Krauts and Japs. Harry,
come back from the Navy, delivered Wonder Bread
to get ahead while you delivered one, two, three, four
more fat loaves steaming from the oven.

For eight years Mark and I were Catholic brats
together at St. Pete's. The Sisters of St. Joseph,
with their black habits and white wimples, sharp
tongues and flat bosoms, rapped the fat blue
catechism over our heads.
> Q. Who made us?
> A. God made us.
> Q. Why did He make us?
> A. To show forth His goodness in this world and share
>   with us His happiness in the next.

Machinegun-style, our alcoholic pastor spat out the Latin
of the Mass: "Introibo ad altare Dei." And, hands folded,
Mark and I fired back: "Ad Dei qui laetificat juventutem
meam." It was not the ideal preparation for life the cataclysm.

At twenty-three, I was still in school, looking for answers
in the books, while Mark, nobody's fool but his own,
had dropped out and drove a milk truck. That brilliant

TRANSITIONS

May day now how many years ago, when it rolled over
and he ignited, slicking four lanes of interstate with milk,
you flipped. They wrapped him in bandages and laid
him in a hospital, and when you stood over him,
weeping, this sudden mummy your son, always
a clown, stuck out his tongue at you and died.

At the funeral while Harry tried to hold us together
("Buck up, now, buck up!" he commanded), you cried
buckets and couldn't extinguish your grief. Now every
time I show up, after all these years, standing in front
of you a substitute son, a scrub off the bench, you cry
your eyes out till you're blind.

Della, it's no sin to cry. You're sixty-two, and I'm old
enough to be your first-born and know better. Mother,
for pity's sake, hold on: while I hang from your breast,
your eyes downcast like a virgin's, and all about us
the leafless summer broils.

III. WHERE ARE WE GOING?

Poem in Uncertain Rhythm

Her husky breath, her lovely voice
come to him this morning, stiffen
his groin like whipped egg whites.

Trying to work this morning
at his desk, all morning burning
in the Jeanne d'Arc flame
of the words she spoke, self
immolating, her breath a perfume
in dizzying drafts.

Mesmerized, not remembering
a thing she said last night,
just the music of her voice purring,
a cat, yes, purely cat sheathing
the clawed voice.

Uncertain how or what to go on,
perhaps some day possessing her,
magic creature, top to toe: tipping
finally after the most slow languorous
kisses and massages along the calf
the thigh the beaded spine the ass
her fire-tilted all-surrounding womb.

WHERE ARE WE GOING?

Meditation for a Chilly February

The cat sits chittering
on the window sill still
gazing at the starlings
in the branches of the plum.
Sits snapping at the huddling
aviary, quick black and you might
think unpalatable snack, flitting
from one branch to another.
Sits on the sill, jaw involuntarily
twitching, brain imprinting prey.

Last summer I climbed
a ladder through the plum
tree thorns, no Christ for
Christ sake, no saint, up
and up the long aluminum
ladder, caulk gun in hand,
a matter of pure practicality.
I was going up to seal an eave's-
trough hole where a squirrel
had gnawed her way inside
and she and her babies nested.
I lusted for nothing less than
sheer rodenticide, to drive all
squirrelly life off the property,
away from the corner of the house
above my study where transcendency
like this muttering, in an easy chair,
is secularly enacted, on a daily basis.

Sits chittering on the cherry sill,
jaws quivering spasmodically
at the possibility of starling snack,
snap, crunch, and gristle of bird

TRANSITIONS

bone, feather, marrow, a narrow,
temporal world, you and I
might say, and yet, apparently,
tasty.

WHERE ARE WE GOING?

Rx for a Painless Enough Life

Take two X-ACTOs,
don't get any sleep,
and see if you can see
anything in the morning,
e.g., monsters! tremblings!
tumbling down flights
of endless Spanish Stairs!
turning on the Spanish
rack and screw!

Certainly, friends, these
fantasies may be regrettable,
a wish to do ourselves entirely
in before life comes along
and we're undone,
peeled like a midwinter
New Zealand plum, then
popped into some monster's
mouth! "I saw his teeth!
I glimpsed annihilation!"

Amen, amen, I say unto you
guys, better to pluck out
both your eyes, hack off
the scrotum, rip out the
ovum, fling 'em into the sea,
than hang around a crappy
job, just one possibility
for not being happy.

Ready

Getting ready to return this body
to the earth. Putting one flattening
foot in front of the other. Awaiting
marching orders. Whipping this body,
trunk and limbs and head, that capital
organ, into Jell-O pudding, a fabric
softening in the whirling dryer
of the sun. Even this hair, long
vainly considered the "crowning
glory," is fading, or "maturing,"
as my "hair artist" says. "Say
 'graying,'" I say to her. "Say
'You're getting ready to return
your body to the earth.'" The eye,
the same muddy blue eye it's always
been, steadies, looks at her, blonde,
maybe thirty, flitty as a black-capped
chickadee, twittering as she goes
about her business in the branches
of the hair. Now, with the privilege
that age confers, positively staring:
not from lust, at last, but a far more
desperate desire: to get someone
besides, beside the self to know
that this too is sweet, this taking off,
this sloughing of the skin, the hair,
the brightness, the glory of the world,
the weight of care.

WHERE ARE WE GOING?

Navel

One summer night
twenty, thirty years
after last sailing
into church nave,
rowing the slow
boat of meditation
on the hopelessness
of his situation, he
pulled past a vast
Chartres cathedral,
so it seemed, anchored
in gleaming light,
womb's illumination
spilling out.

Apart then instantly
from temporal doubt,
glimpsed through
wide flung portals
an altar bathed
in candlelight,
instantaneously
altered once more:
a floating child,
luminous isle,
sea creature rocked
in trance and tide,
uprooted, all things
left behind.

It was just a passing
moment. He did not
drop to his knees,
conversion mystery.

Afterwards he felt
foolish enough: it
was only a moment
floating, washed
amnioticly by
night's unexpectedly
quickened air.

WHERE ARE WE GOING?

Night Thoughts

Not sleeping, with my wife, in our king
size Beautyrest, a kingdom of emptiness
between us, I rise at 3 a.m. to occupy
my brown study. In the dim light
of a reading lamp, goosenecked
in a screaming manufactory,
I read Robert Lowell's "Topless"
poem and think of you:
how I've wanted to bray my
jackass lusts, in what might
only be new timbres of sterility,
and say, "I've got something for you,
girl — a warm heart and hard cock."
As if that's anything to crow about.
Half the world goes to sleep each night,
the four-chambered blood pump pumping
blood to all parts of the body till,
in the small hours of the morning,
glory blossoms on the autonomic vine
and lust's sweet tendrils glut the hand.

Two Views of Love

"Each sucked a secret, and each wore a mask." — George
Meredith, Modern Love

1.
The fat man has a crush on my wife.
He eyes her trim waistline, her luscious
breasts, more than a mouthful and not
to be wasted. He wants to curl around her,
a boa constrictor, a chubby tuba, making
beautiful music with her all night long.
The coils of his instrument crush, oh so
tenderly, the small breath out of the gazelle.
All night long, all night long, bubbling
sad man music, the woman disappearing,
incredibly, into the tiny mouthpiece
and emerging, incredibly, as sad iridescent
bubbles of champagne music.

2.
The slim young man desires her too,
slithering green mamba and ruby tongue,
across the whispering grasses. This jive
devil has her mesmerized through the long
hot afternoons, glazed at the bright red apple
and the long flickering ruby tongue.
What he whispers, what he murmurs
only the grasses hear and her mole-tipped
delicate ear. Would she run, would she,
fixed by the long forked tongue.

WHERE ARE WE GOING?

Poem on the Beautiful Hands of Jennifer

In the half-light of the marriage bed
you take from under the sheets and show me
your incredibly beautiful hands —
small, slim, tapering into flame —
and hold me then to the heat of your breast,
your heart which is choiring in this milky
light, and tell me with your erotically
articulate fingers how close we can be.
As I unfurl from doubt's tight fist,
from the fetal dark, it dawns on me
how wholly unclenched and open you are —
your fingers which know so well how to sew
and cook and tease a balky piano into music
and stroke a lover ecstatically, a wand
of subtle light and heat that binds me gently
to you, this early hour of the morning,
in the half-light of the marriage bed.

Walking the Plank

Little did he know, that March evening
how many years ago, after their first date
(a movie, bowling, sodas at the drive-in)
when he walked her down the two-by-tens
her father had thrown across the muddy
yard after the tornado had wrought its
destruction that he'd be marching her
up the aisle a few short years thereafter.

Little did he know when he walked her
down those planks in that muddy yard,
when under the wheeling stars of spring
they stopped at the door, dizzy with new
love, and embracing, kissed once, no twice,
long and hungrily on the lips, and he told
her he could hold her in his arms forever.

For soon they'd be leaving the snug slip
of family, careening together the high seas
of marriage, lurching wildly with love, falling
out into piratical practice: have at each other
with jealousy's saber, stab in the back
with vengeance's dagger, hoist the skull
and crossbones of others' affections
over each other's heart.

As if each might feel compelled, blindfolded
and alone, to step out on the plank and say
a last prayer over a shark-maddened sea.

WHERE ARE WE GOING?

Lone Star State

Emerging hand in hand from the subway,
we make our way toward the St. Moritz on the Park,
where we'll stay a week (one-oh-eight per night),
take in the Metropolitan, see *Love's Labor's Lost,*
groove to late-night jazz uptown, smoking
and drinking just enough to feel a bit wicked.

Two years married, we're happy as two hares,
bounding out of Texas for the Big Apple.
Lone stars, we shine in this twilit city,
twang like the music of the Southern spheres.
When we look up from our map (the moon sliced
like a peach above Manhattan), a native of these parts
materializes to give friendly directions: left here,
two blocks, then right, and you are there.

We thank this courteous stranger, hurry on, pull
up short a block from the hotel: on the sidewalk
at our feet, dead as a picture at an exhibition,
the body of a young man, maybe twenty,
gouts of brain flung like seed in the moonlight,
a splintered four-by-four beam in the road.
Across the avenue, construction workers,
miniscule and high up on a new building,
look down like visitors from another planet.

The police, already on the scene, talk to witnesses,
take notes. An ambulance pulls up, the corpse
is hustled off, the crowd disperses murmuring.
I look my new wife in the hazel eye and see motes
swirling like the nebulae. Chilled to the bone
I kiss her faultless cheek, and we hurry on.

Drought and Desire

A dry July, summer in drydock, all keels high
and dry, all bets off. Two wives, two friends
on the dry deck, gin-and-tonics clinking
and the Swede photographer proposes, "Let's
drink to the drought!" stopping down his friend's
wife in the narrowed light, bringing up chances
of rain. "My old lady got six inches last night."
"Poked her twice?" *Amo, amas, amat,* I love
her inundated twat. Two friends, two wives,
the season's ginsoaked ship sailing high seas.
All night, lightning flickers. They go home
and launder an old argument. Ozone,
spilt like spiritual bleach, stings the tub
of the heavens. Thunder's not been heard
like that since they met and conjugated desire
("I fuck, you fuck, he/she/it fucks, we all
fuck our ever-loving brains out"), becoming
one with, inane as, the angels, supercerebral
and riding the clouds. Sudden sheets of rain
snap like sheets on the line. The conjugal bed
crackles. Two sheets to the gale, pitching
on the wet deck, they roll and haw and explode
when he says, "You'd like him to fuck you with me?"

WHERE ARE WE GOING?

Encounter

The dog days done, in the sudden sweet cool
of the August evening, Charlie, my high
stepping Lakeland, and I step into the pool
of the breeze. Leashed and choke-chained,
he prances the blocks of Georgian houses,
large squat square wood and stucco houses
built to host turn-of-the-century dreams,
heels indifferently to my itinerary, marks
the trees, squats at the curb and evacuates.
My mind, already satisfactorily empty,
far from Sirius, is borne aloft, a punt,
a shell, and skims the seminal shoals
of the stars. Now, as my terrier noses
the earth, a bitch part Lab, part every
dogsniff in the city, explodes from
the shadows. And, in her wake, her
pretty mistress, young, trim, jeaned,
blonde and bobbed, her towheaded
six-year-old boy in tow.

Therese, she says, giving her hand.
Greg, I say, and we stand in the pooled
dark talking, her house gleaming behind us,
now aluminum clad, the American dream abating
but the winters' heat bills low, she says, her marriage
gleaming behind her, her ex-husband a dirty mutt.
Lunging and panting, her dog throws herself atop my dog.
Sublimating and restrained for once, I drink to her
young flesh only with mine eyes — stand on
the whirling pavement, inhaling the earth,
suddenly transfixed as a statue or a star.

Szczecin University Choir Storms Holy Cross

The girls in Mary-blue, surpliced dresses,
the boys in black tuxes, the maestro tuxed
and precise, jittery as a swallow feeding
its young, his tongue too darting direction
to his brood of forty-some young Poles,
doing the U.S.A. for the first time.

Everyone sweltered in the ninety-eight-
degree heat, the parish auditorium a Turkish
bath crammed with antique Polish-Americans
and that fresh angels' flesh booming songs
of faith — the Latin Mass, Polish folk
tunes, Negro spirituals in quaint accent.

I picked out one in the beam of libido,
seraphic soprano who soloed, haloed
in cascades of dark, dark Rapunzel hair,
and in my mind's eye's mote climbed her,
parting each hair to get at the toothed star
of her twat. Everyone gorging on pot luck
afterward, in the church basement — Polish
sausage and cherry tart, sweet punch and coffee —
amid a grotesquerie of pensioned flesh, she
stood on tiptoe, angel in tight white pants now
and tee-shirt, and kissed a blond tenor's angel lips.

WHERE ARE WE GOING?

My Friends the Artists Dream

Tommy Wadd carves and Emmy quilts. She barks,
he nickers. When in hell will you ever earn
some money! she yells. Emmy and I kiss long
and furiously, while Tommy works obliviously
on his O'Keefe/Nevelson piece. It's a lozenge
shaped coffin that you open and then a blue sky
patched with cotton clouds explodes. The head
of Napoleon sits on top, gazing apoplectically.
Emmy takes me up the stairs and there in her
and Tommy's bedroom, under her latest quilt,
Buffalo Bill on a milk white steed ("Howdy
folks!"), Annie Oakley with six shooters blazing,
Sitting Bull and the ghost buffalo, we do it,
screw it about as tight as you can make it,
nail down the lid with a final yelp or two.
Napoleon, his big gaze booming, is choking
on the tongue Tommy has chiseled in. The coffin
sags with a flat black glaze. The sky pours pennies.

The Lover's First Taste of Extraconnubial Bliss

Mmmmmmmm, Ms. Brown
body, the taste of
your flat Bulgarian
belly, your fat

dappled thighs,
your arching ass:
they all fit so
nicely in my

hands, eyes,
mouth and
isn't it a
shame that

we can't go on
and on like this
world without
end, amen?

But then it's late,
your hair is
flecked with gray,
what would my

wife, your husband
say? and both of
us must rise to
work tomorrow.

Still, s'il vous
plaît, Ms. Brown
body, save me a
place at the last

WHERE ARE WE GOING?

supper of your
ass, thighs,
belly, lips and
labia: faithful

to this end
to eat you and
be your fond
communicant.

El Rey de Mi Corazon

The signs at the Museo de Antropologia
warn *No Tocar,* don't touch. Behind red
velvet rope I gape at the round brown
Toltec earth mothers, pyramids for tits
and holes for seeds.

In this filthy capital the smog's so bad
that, a block away, I can hardly see
the gold monuments of angels, martyrs
of the revolution, crooked politicians.
Monolingual and jittery, I feel the pinch
of beggars, conmen, thieves. In this melting
pot of races, this piss/shit/fuck pot
of twenty million, fertility is at rolling boil.

On every other street corner, her back
against a marble office tower, an Indian
woman squats, a baby at her fat brown tit,
a mitt out begging tourists and mestizos
for *monedas,* two, three other brats circling.

After a week of churches, pyramids, museums,
dirt, I've seen enough of the show. Blind-drunk
one night in the Zona Rosa, where, fair game,
all good Yankees go, I hire not one but two *putas.*
We haggle, and as we settle for a hundred fifty
bucks the fake blonde sings, *"Si, mi amor,* I love
you *absolutamente, rey de mi corazon."*
In the taxi to the tart hotel, the brunette offers
me her sweet *chichis,* feels my cock harden
under her hand, exclaims, *"Maxissimo!"*

WHERE ARE WE GOING?

Red and black flocked wallpaper, red and black
bedspread, I'm fucked if I can get it up again.
I diddle one girl and the other giggles and cracks
jokes (I'm getting every peso's worth), strokes
me while I jiggle like a minnow on a hook.
Then they shower together, and, furled in my
red/white/blue underwear, a dirty American flag,
I smoke.

Light mesh of limbs, feet and fingers, toes and hands,
we lie abed afterwards talking and the whores pronounce
"el miembro muerte. Little Maximilian's dead," they say,
"kaput, shot in the head." They say I'm a very nice man
though I don't believe in God: *"No crees!"*: and bite
a bit more than is strictly necessary: "Why you like
that *mordir?*" Unlike most of their johns, Mexican men,
I don't insist on fucking all night long, and when
the pretty brunette tells me, as we're kissing one
last time, I have a rare "intellectual culture," puritan
Yankee that I am, I almost jump out of my skin.

Onan Suite

1. Seeding the Dark

Fourteen years old and
lonely as a loon I found
myself in a semenary in
Ohio where the priests

(lucky if they didn't hurt
themselves) sported
monstrous brass crosses
in their cinctures.

One hundred freshmen
bunking in a huge dorm
room we were adjured to
keep the magna silentia

all night long. The
only sounds we heard
were the ghostly
strains of Gregorian

chant floating up
from the chapel where
the priests were
choiring and the

sounds we made in our
bunks like boats
rowing (the scrape of
oar against oarlock,

WHERE ARE WE GOING?

the slap of wave on
hull) to an ecstatic
shore: all through
the great silence

one hundred teenage
boys their heads
ringing with Latin
their bodies aflame

rowing their boats
ashore (the river
Eros sunny and
wide): alleluia!

2. Ecce Homo

He's a two-fisted
man who can change
hands without missing
a stroke; is intimate

with the girls in
the club, Mary
Fist and Rosy Palm;
can hold his own

with the best of
them; is adept
at beating the meat,
choking the chicken,

bleeding the weasel,
jerking the gherkin,
and other acts of what
we like to call self

abuse. As a teenager
he was studious,
jerking off not till
he went blind but

just till he needed
glasses. He knows
that in the puritan
lexicon haste makes

paste and is a heinous
crime. Now that he's
married and has a
respectable job, he

WHERE ARE WE GOING?

wouldn't be caught
dead doing what we'd
kill to catch him at.
While 95 percent admit

they do, he's joined the 5
percent who lie. Friends,
I wash my hands of the
matter. Behold the man.

3. Look Ma No Hands

Hands bound to my
side like Odysseus to
the mast, fifteen
years old and prone

to excess, I lie face
down upon the mattress,
eyes closed, ears
plugged, seeing and

hearing no evil. My
body starts to move
like a smooth canoe
through creeks and

lakes of purewhite
lilies. Nubile forms
of women rise
glisteningly nude

all about me, a
classical gallery:
heads lopped, no
hands, breasts

veined with pink,
moons round, profound
cracks where my eye
plunges, tons

of noble marble
floating on the
water. A drunken
boat rocking, a

WHERE ARE WE GOING?

fish hooked and
leaping, its pale
belly, its flaming
gills, its throat

slit: talk to me,
baby, tell me
your dumb
anonymous name.

4. Transitional

Of course there was
pleasure, and terror,
and irremediable
guilt. I looked at

the plaster virgin
in the church nave,
dumb as fish and
sorrowful as grapes,

and ducked into the
confessional. Usually
the priest would hand
out a ton of Our

Fathers and Hail
Marys and a few Glory
Bes to boot. For
Christ and penance

sake I don't know if
I ever really got it
up, for even while I
was bleaching the old

soul with prayer I'd
be licking my lips
over which of the
neighborhood girls

I'd be beating off
to that night: Dolly
with the heart
shaped ass, June

WHERE ARE WE GOING?

with the deep
gray eyes, Sandra
with the come
hither laughter. Oh!

I could go on and
on counting the ways,
telling the beads
of my onanistic rosary,

a sly and unrepentant
teenage Catholic boy
who could never quite
make it across.

5. Songs My Mother Taught Me

What was I, already
sweet sixteen, when
my dear old mother
took me aside and

said, Gregory, God
gave women breasts
to attract men, there'll
come a day when the Lord

will cover you at night
with pollution. I
looked at her curiously
and grinned, the breasts

I'd sucked as an infant
sagging, the face with its
wrinkles, and kept
good counsel to myself:

how I'd made note
already of the jugs of
the ladies (brimming
with or without milk for

their babies), how
I'd already come like
Noah to the ark and
taking on board all

the animals, male and
female in phantasmagoric
pairs, damn near drowned
in my own semen.

WHERE ARE WE GOING?

6. Gloria

Under the scintillating
stars, the wide canopy
of heaven, two a.m., I
stepped out on the porch

and shot my gism into
the garden. Damn that
lovely girl, Gloria, who
brought me to such fever

pitch and then no no no
no, she said, no no no
no, be a good boy.
Hanging their heads,

immaculate white bells,
the lilies of the valley
steamed with my unplanted
seed. A lovely Japanese

American girl, she every
time I came to see her
saw that I came alone,
her quicksand kisses

sucking me in, and went
in essential confusion.
Out on the porch,
miniscule me, under the

stars' flaming canopy, I
shot my wad, looked up,
and saw the Dog Star
bucking.

TRANSITIONS

7. Sweet Solitude

Accompanied only by
thoughts of one I love
or lust madly after, her
perfect form swaying,

I'm down on my knees
again groaning as
if praying, my groin
shooting fires of

enchantment. When
I reach out I touch
not this cantatrice
but only my

self and my throw
away youth. Those
days are long
gone yet I hang

onto them, my teddy
bear, my blanket, my
tiddly winks, my
titty, the daily

orange my mother feeds
me, horsing me up
and down on her
knee. But this is

stupid, clutching
such poppets, and
finally I cry out
in despair, the

WHERE ARE WE GOING?

song having
vanished into thin
air, no no no no, I just
want to be aloin.

Charms of Oblivion

This rubber band around the wrist
reminds us of something we forget.
The notes scribbled on envelopes
mirror once more an evanescence.
The smudged asterisk on the calendar.
The dog-eared corner of the book.
If only we could put our hand on it.

Something volatile as water,
airy as blue sky. Something
that consumes like fire, asphyxiates
like earth. Something elemental,
out of sight, that whines and burrows
in the night and yet is not quite
out of mind. Something subterranean
that soils its own bed. Something
ineluctable that sits on its own head.

If only these charms, these talismans,
led somewhere. If only there were
a back door.

ENDNOTES

"Perverse Streak." All first poems, in the three sections of this book, are about poetry; that is, they play with and enact, or reenact, the process of creating poetry.

"Baby Narcisse." So begins a skein of family poems, more or less based on fact. What provoked this particular titbit I don't know. Was I close to my mom, Mary Zeck? My very first memory of life on earth is being dandled on her knee. RIP, Mary Mahala Zeck, mother, cook, bridge-player, dancer, gardener, and life of the party.

"Enfants Terribles." My little brother Bob and I had a love-hate relation. He was just 15 months younger and somehow, all too often, got in the way. If you have sibs, you might know how that goes. RIP, Bob.

"Formicary." This too is a true story, or something like true. That is, I remember this story of my younger sister Kathy, or Kit, or think I do, as one of those perverse ineradicable anthems of childhood.

"Bachelors' Camp." Here I ventriloquize, assuming what I hope is a fair copy of my wife Jennifer's voice or tone as a teenager in a story that belongs to her.

"Variation on a Theme by Maxim Gorky." Gorky's *My Childhood* is a book of fond and cruel remembrances of life in a Russian village. Gorky recalls, among other things, how his grandfather would beat him nearly to death and his grandmother entertain him with romantic and spiritual songs and stories from village life.

"Dithyramb." A dithyramb, according to dictionary.com, is "1) a Greek choral song or chant of vehement or wild character and of usually irregular form, originally in honor of Dionysus or Bacchus; 2) any poem or other composition having similar characteristics, as an impassioned or exalted theme or irregular form; 3) any wildly enthusiastic speech or writing." Brother Bob died at age 46 of alcoholism. This poem commemorates more or less accurately one of the equally painful and comical episodes of his career in the bottle.

"Blood Brothers." Don't know what I was thinking or drinking, but this story must've come out of an anthropological account in the newspaper. Forgive me for being so old and not yet wise.

"Eden in Monochrome." Our son Gabriel had a high school friend whose black brother died tragically as recounted here. I simply kidnaped the story and made it my own

"First Love." Good thing I didn't marry this gal, right? She was a perfectly warm and talented person. What can I say? I've just said it.

"Dedication." As a junior at the University of Minnesota, I attended a poetry reading by Robert Creeley, a poet of what was called the Black Mountain School. My friend and fraternity brother Robert (Irving) Black (*In hoc signo vinces*) had given me a copy of Creeley's book *Words* and inscribed it as indicated here. RIP, both Roberts: Creeley died of lung disease in 2005, and Black, the old friend, with whom I re-established contact after 50 years, died of complications of Covid-19 in 2020. I didn't know Irving long enough the second time around to learn whether he had in fact fled to poetry as his citadel.

"Epithalamion." According to dictionary.com, an epithalamion is "a song or poem in honor of a bride and bridegroom." What drives us to dream of what we cannot have? Brother Bob, who worked in the healthcare professions and had a flair for self-dramatization, called himself, from time to time, "Billy Bob

ENDNOTES

McGruder" or "Billy Biff McGruder." January 22 was his birthday.

"Minneapolis Is Empty Now." Brother Gerry was almost eight years my elder, a lustful, thoughtful, artistic inventor, a wonderful photographer and illustrator, who for a time ran a nude-photography studio called "Le Corps de Lumière." He was also a geographer with a Ph.D. from UCLA and knew about land and water masses; he talked about water with a mystical sense of wonder and possibility.

"Prayer for a Life without Tools." Like Gerry in Minneapolis, I bought a big clapboard house in St. Paul. These old monsters were hell to keep up.

"Mote and Beam." I remember reading this poem to brother Bob when we were visiting my retired parents in Cherokee Village, Arkansas. He laughed like hell at it, as he saw, I think, that both he and I were the butts of this brotherly-love joke.

"No Muse." Our son Gabe must've popped in on me in my office on Lincoln Ave. in St. Paul. He would have been 15 years old round about 1988. Do you remember those old computer monitors with green type on black background? Mine was part of a Televideo computer system, and the OS was, gods forgive us, CP/M. I was doing freelance business writing on this thing at a time when MS-DOS had not yet established dominance.

"Maine Summer." With gratitude and apologies to Ellen Goodman. This poem is based on one of her columns reprinted, no doubt, in the *Star Tribune* or *Pioneer Press,* our Twin Cities' newspapers. I manage here to sneak in a line from Ralph Waldo Emerson's poem "Each and All": "Nothing is fair or good alone," a poem that also recounts, with a Transcendental slant, the expropriation of objects from nature.

"Revolutionary." Pieter is a Dutch friend, whom I met at a theater production in the late 1970s while he and I were teaching, he as guest, I as untenured assistant professor, at Wayne State University in Detroit.

"In Praise of Privies." I found the makings of this poem in Witold Rybczynski's *Home: A Short History of an Idea* (1987), then reworked, reassembled, spat on, and polished 'em.

"Another Minneapolis Poem." James Wright, who taught briefly at the University of Minnesota in the 1950s, wrote "A Minneapolis Poem," which my poem plays off. For Wright's text, go to www.poetryfoundation.com. Wright was associated with my high school English teacher William Duffy and Robert Bly, founders of *The Fifties* and then *The Sixties* literary magazine. Yes, the William Duffy of "Lying in a Hammock on William Duffy's Farm near Pine Island, Minnesota." That William Duffy. Who taught English, as I say, in the 1960s at the Christian Brothers' Benilde High School, St. Louis Park, Minnesota, which I attended from 1962 to 1965, and as far as I know is still living, in St. Paul, "lively as a wild chicken," according to an account published recently by Minnesota Public Radio.

"Two Birds in the News." This is a found poem based on photos and captions in the newspaper of 17 June 1987.

"Conductor." My father's father was a family legend even in life. He left the farm near St. Cloud, Minnesota when only twelve years old, as he was unable to get along with his stepfather, and moved to Minneapolis. Since his death in 1968, Anthony Szczech (the original family surname) has grown only more poignant and tragicomical. The Polish word *gówno* means shit.

"Guinness Book Record Proposed." I found this story found in the newspaper on or about 6 December 1988.

ENDNOTES

"Birthday Wish for My Father." My father, Robert E. Zeck, and Mother Mary retired in the summer of 1978 to Cherokee Village, Arkansas. My father turned 75 in that place on 2 July 1988. I was living then in St. Paul, Minnesota in the three-story four-square mentioned in "Prayer for a Life without Tools."

"Something for My Cousin." My first cousin Darlene died at her own hand in March 1989. Her twin brother Duane had died years earlier of a rare blood disorder. May the star-crossed twins rest in peace.

"Photos from an Album Never Opened." This one is about the death of my best friend, Mark Shuck. As an undergrad at the University of Minnesota, I housed with him and three or four other students. At this point in his life Mark was perhaps more interested in partying than studying and was working for the PO. He would go out on his postal route, punch out at noon, loll in the sun and drink beer, then clock back in just to check out.

"Meditation for a Chilly February." A tribute to our cat Ms. Green, who in her early years would peer out the dining room window of our Lincoln Ave. house in St. Paul, tormented by the birds in the plum tree. She lived to be nineteen or twenty, and is buried in a wooden coffin in the yard of a subsequent house.

"Rx for a Painless Enough Life." Great Caesar's ghost, where did this come from! Was I reading comic books? Chatting with our son Gabe? Dreaming? Drinking? And how do I order another fantasy of this kind?

"Ready." Philosophy and poetry, too, are cheaper and better than beauty and vanity, aren't they? *Vita brevis,* as they say, or did say, *ars longa* (life is short, art is long).

TRANSITIONS

"Navel." I'd been downtown St. Paul one summer evening, perhaps with friends, and saw the doors of a church flung wide open, the nave and altar revealed, and light spilling out on the pavement. This was the small, ornate Church of St. Louis, King of France, built in 1868 to minister to the French-speaking population of the area.

"Night Thoughts." Speaking of Robert Lowell, whose *Life Studies* I read in grad school in Texas, there may be some parallels between his interests and methods and my own in these early confessional poems. Not that I can take any credit for his influence or for Robert Creeley's. RIP, both Roberts.

"Two Views of Love." Ah, jealousy in marriage, where would we be without it? On our own, I suppose, with no one to be jealous of.

"Lone Star State." Must've read about this accident in a newspaper story. My bride and I did not make it to New York, in fact, till we'd been married 45 years.

"Drought and Desire." No comment.

"Encounter." We lived in St. Paul near several colleges, and it was common for me to see or meet attractive co-eds or neighbors on my walk with our Lakeland terrier, Charlie, who just about always would pull up as I eyed the women lustily, put on the brakes, and take a dump.

"Szczecin University Choir Storms Holy Cross." Holy Cross was the Polish church just a few blocks down from Grandpa Tony's place in "Nordeast" Minneapolis. It was the church that my grandfather, grandmother, and the three sons attended.

"My Friends the Artists Dream." Based on a true story, as they say. Does that make it any less reprehensible or delicious? Hey, it's a dream.

ENDNOTES

"Onan Suite." In the 1980s, when I'd returned to the Twin Cities, I played Sunday tennis doubles with Ted Wright as my partner (against the cunning and wily old duo of Jon Wendt and Eric Watkins) and exchanged poems with Ted. Friend, scholar, poet, mentor, and, later, in retirement, English Professor Emeritus at the University of Minnesota, Ted was delighted with this suite. What can I say? It's a man thing, you might not understand.

"Charms of Oblivion." My dad, the lawyer, Robert E. Zeck, who died in Arkansas, February 2008, kept rubber bands around his wrist and scribbled notes on envelopes he'd cut open from his legal practice.